Mamma Toppers
Funny Sandwichbook

by Patricia Olivia Stewer

PIFFZ

www.piffz.com

Mamma Toppers Funny Sandwichbook
© Piffz, 2016
www.piffz.com

1. edition, 1. printing
Printed in EU 2016

ISBN 978-87-93084-25-4

© 2016 Author: Patricia Olivia Stewer

Cover and graphic design:
Yummp Design Studio - www.yummp.net

 PIFFZ

Index

Sandwich bread

Sandwich bread

INGREDIENTS

25 g margarine

300 g of milk

25 g of yeast

1 tbsp sugar

1 tsp salt

500 g flour

Homemade
is the best!

PREPARATION

Melt margarine and add the milk
and yeast.
Add salt, sugar and flour until dough
is smooth.

Cover dough and let rise for 25
minutes
Press dough into a
flat rectangle. Roll into a sausage and
place it in a bread tin.

Cover the tin with aluminum foil
Let dough rise until it reaches the
edge of the tin.

Preheat the oven to 200°C degrees.
Remove foil and bake the bread in
center of oven for about 30 minutes.
Take it out of the tin and roll it into a
clean dish towel and let it cool.

Shellfish salad

Shellfish Salad

INGREDIENTS

125 g shrimp into small cubes

6-8 crab sticks

Dill (fresh or dried)

Salt and pepper

4-6 tbsp Good mayonnaise

(preferably homemade)

PREPARATION

Crabsticks Cut into small cubes.
Mix the shrimp into small cubes and
add a lot of dill.

Mix it all together with a good
mayonnaise and season with
salt and pepper.

Sausage Salad

Sausage Salad

INGREDIENTS

2 large potatoes

8-10 sausages

4-6 tbsp mayonnaise

1 tbsp Dijon mustard

1 small onion

2 tbsp chives

1 tbsp sugar

Salt and pepper

PREPARATION

Boil the potatoes and let them cool down
then cut into small cubes.
Cut the sausages into thin slices.

Dressing:

Chop the onion into fine cubes and then finely chop chives.
Mix mayonnaise, Dijon mustard, sugar, onion and chives and taste it with salt and pepper.

Add the cooled boiled potatoes and sausage slices and let the salad stand to cool down until serving.

Egg-Ham salad

Egg-Ham salad

INGREDIENTS

6 eggs

1 package sliced ham
or a large piece of ham.

fresh parsley

Salt and pepper

4-6 tbsp Good mayonnaise

(preferably homemade)

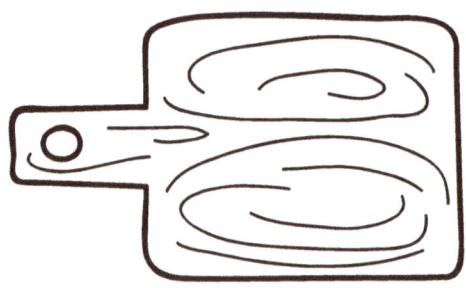

PREPARATION

Boil the eggs and let them cool.

Then cut them into cubes

Cut the ham into very fine cubes. Mix it with eggs.

Chop the fresh parsley and mix in.

Mix it all together with a good mayonnaise and taste with salt and pepper.

Salmon salad

Salmon salad

INGREDIENTS

400 g baked salmon (cold)

200 g smoked salmon, diced

3 scallions, thinly sliced

Salt and pepper

4-6 tbsp Good mayonnaise

(preferably homemade)

PREPARATION

Pull the cold baked salmon into
small pieces with your fingers.

Mix it with the smokedsalmon into
small

cubes and the sliced scallions.

Mix it all together with a good
mayonnaise and taste with
salt and pepper.

Chicken-Bacon salad

Chicken-Bacon salad

INGREDIENTS

1 cold grilled chicken fillet

1 package of bacon

2 slices of pineapple

onions

curry

Salt and pepper

4-6 tbsp Good mayonnaise

(preferably homemade)

PREPARATION

Cut chicken into small cubes.

Roast the bacon cubes and let them cool.Chop them a second time with a knife.

Cut pineapple into small cubes. Cut the onion into small cubes. Mix it all together.

Mix a good mayonnaise with a little pineapple juice and curry powder and taste with salt and pepper.

Mix it with chicken mixture.

Tuna salad

Tuna salad

INGREDIENTS

2 cans of tuna in oil

½ red bell pepper

1 small can of corn

1 handful of peas

onion

Salt and pepper

4-6 tbsp Good mayonnaise

(preferably homemade)

PREPARATION

Cut red pepper into fine pieces and then cut the onions finely.

Mix tuna, red pepper, corn, peas and onions together in a bowl.

Mix it all with a good mayonnaise and taste with salt and pepper.

Chicken-capers salad

Chicken-capers salad

INGREDIENTS

1 cold grilled chicken fillet

2 tbsp capers

2 large pickled cucumbers

onions

Salt and pepper

4-6 tbsp Good mayonnaise

(preferably homemade)

PREPARATION

Cut chicken into small cubes.

Chop capers finely.

Cut the cucumbers into small cubes.

Cut the onion into small cubes. Mix it all together.

Then add a good mayonnaise and taste with salt and pepper.

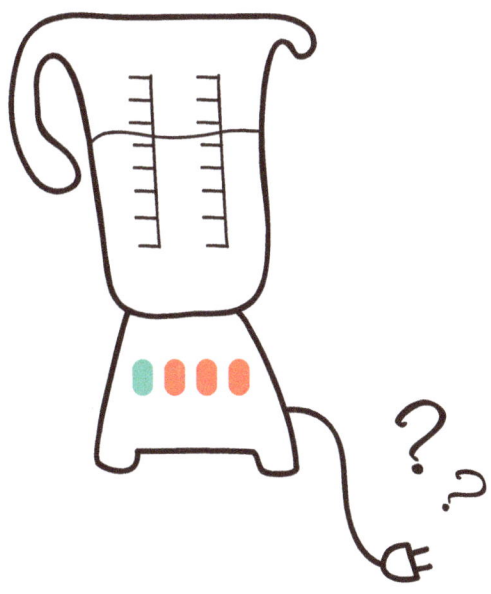

Notessssssssssssss

We need milk!